MW01115588

This journal belongs to:

_____

"...The effectual fervent prayer of a righteous woman availeth much."
James 5:16

Fierce Femme:

You are a warrior;
Powerful, purposeful and
influential.
Your femininity is a gift and a
strength.
Your prayers have the power to
transform, transcend and
triumph over the enemy.
Own it and use it for God's glory!

Celi Marie Dean-Touré

HOW TO USE THIS PRAYER JOURNAL

This prayer and vision journal were created with you in mind: *Fierce Femme.* A space where you can write out your prayers, express your gratitude, keep track of prayer requests, record important revelations, write down your dreams, testimonies, visions and heart desires.

This journal is divided into FIVE SECTIONS:

- Her Prayers
- Her Praises
- Her Intercessions
- Her Dreams
- Her Visions

Each section was created to help keep you organized while also giving you the freedom and flexibility to be creative and to personalize this journal so that it reflects you.

Over the next few pages you will find some examples of how to use these sections and a brief description as to why each section was chosen for this journal. One of the features that I love are the blank pages at the end designed for you to create mini-monthly vision boards!

HER GAME CHANGING STRATEGY IS PRAYER Journal is a reminder that amidst all the grind, prayer is essential. We can have the greatest ideas, strategies, etc. but if we are not making time for God- to pray and cover those ideas- we are doing ourselves and the visions and people we've been assigned to a disservice.

Prayer is a form of self-care. It's how we release and refocus. We gain our strength, confidence, wisdom and direction through prayer.

Most importantly it's how we communicate and invest in our relationship with God. Prayer is our weapon in times of warfare, our peace in times of distress, and our source of power in our everyday lives.

As fierce women of God, prayer is a major part of our lifestyle.

her prayers

Good ole pen and paper remains a powerful way to communicate, increase our memory and help to keep us focused. Use this section of the journal to write out your daily prayer, record any significant dreams you had the night before and jot down the scripture you are meditating on.

Quiet yourself, set your mind and heart on Jesus and commit your day into His hands.

Example:

Date: 1/1/19

Father God,

Thank you for this morning. I commit my mind, will and emotions to you. I ask for wisdom to do the work that I need to get done today. Thank you for a productive day, divine connections and favor to get what I need to get done today. I bless your name and thank you for another day to be used by You. In Jesus name, Amen

Dream: In my dream last night I was going around a dark city, laying my hands-on people and praying for them and delivering them. I walked into a room and it was pitch black but there was a table in the middle. When I slammed my hands on the table, I would say "In Jesus name" and the light would flicker. Eventually after hitting my hands on the table three times the entire room lit up and I felt the power of the name "Jesus."

Scripture:

II Timothy 1:7 "For God hath not given us the spirit of fear; but of power, and of love, and of a sound mind."

her praises

An attitude of gratitude will change your life! Just like prayer, praise and worship are powerful and essential to our everyday lives.

Use this section to write down the things you are grateful for.

Be specific.

This is more than just your everyday -Thank you God for waking me up this morning-praise. Write down something that happened that day or something someone did that you are grateful for.

In addition to the everyday gratitude- use this space to record your testimonies and praise reports!

Example:

Date: 1/1/19

I am so grateful today for my husband. He surprised me with a spa date and it was right on time! So grateful for his act of love and thoughtfulness.

Date: 1/10/19

PRAISE REPORT!

Hallelujah!!! Today I received my promotion. I've been praying for this for 2 years and believing God and finally today, He answered my prayer. I got the promo! I've received a raise in my income-and even favor with flexible hours and putting forward a project idea that I had in mind. Thank you, Jesus!!!

her intercessions

"If all your prayers were answered would it change the world or just yours?" - Unknown

Do you ever find yourself promising to pray for someone or certain issues only to forget what the prayer request was or eventually forgetting to pray about it all together?

This section of the journal is a great way to help you remember the prayer requests of others while also holding you accountable to praying for the people you said you would pray for. Use the space to write down prayer requests, name of the person you are praying for, and the date their prayer was answered.

Example:

Date	Name and Request	Date Answered
1/1/19	Elle Fierce	3/5/19
	New job where she can use her gifts and talents and get paid her ideal salary.	
1/2/19	Judah	1/10/19
	Prayer for healing of his body and that he won't need surgery.	
1/3/19	Faith	3/3/22
	Her husband. God connect her with the man He has designed for her and that her husband will recognize her, and she will recognize him.	

her dreams

This is your safe space to write down your BIGGEST PRAYERS and to record the dreams and desires that scare you the most.

Be BOLD!

Circle your prayer, write scriptures related to the prayer request, and be specific.

Think about this as the section to write down all of your dreams and prayers that require a little bit more than a mustard-seed-sized faith!

Example:

New HOME

Thank you, God, for our new home. 4 bedrooms with an office space to run my business, a guest room for family to stay over, and a walk-in closet in the master bedroom. Safe neighborhood on FAVOR street. Move in by next Christmas 2019

Open My Womb!

Thank you, God, that you open my womb to conceive and have a healthy baby who will be filled with joy and love.

"I prayed for this child, and the LORD has granted me what I asked of him."
I SAMUEL 1:27

My husband

God I am believing you for the man you have created to be my life partner. Ephesians 5:20 My husband will love me like Christ loves the church.

her visions

Write the vision and make it plain! Visualizing is powerful and a great reminder of what your goals are so that you can stay focused or get back on track when you become distracted.

You may already have a larger vision board with short term and long-term goals. You can use this section as a fun, creative and effective way to break down your larger vision into monthly goals.

Cut out images and paste or tape them into the journal. Write down affirmations, prayers and words that inspire you. Take out the colored markers, pens, and pencils and use them to draw and express yourself!

Imagination and creativity are things that we think we must let go of when we get older, but we need them! This prayer and vision section is a fun way to use your creativity, release some stress and can be very therapeutic.

Example:

Scripture Index

FAITH
Proverbs 3:5-6
Matthew 6:30
Romans 5:1-2
Hebrews 11

HEALTH/HEALING
Proverbs 3:5-8
Isaiah 53:5
Jeremiah 17:14
Mark 5:34

MARRIAGE
Genesis 2:24
Matthew 19:6
Mark 10:9
Ephesians 5:21-25

PURPOSE
Jeremiah 23:11
Romans 8:28
Philippians 2:3
1 Peter 2:9

FINANCES
Deuteronomy 8:18
Proverbs 3:9-10
Proverbs 22:7
Luke 6:38

BUSINESS
Isaiah 48:17
Proverbs 18:16
Proverbs31:16-18
Colossians 3:23-24

SURRENDER
Matthew 11:28-29
Galatians 2:20
James 4:7
1 Peter 5:6-10

CONFIDENCE
Deuteronomy 31:6
Jeremiah 17:7
Proverbs 3:5-6
Philippians 4:13

ANXIETY
Psalms 94:19
John 14:1
Philippians 4:6-7
Matthew 6:25-34

LOVE
1 Corinthians 13:4-5
Ephesians 4:8
John 15:12
1 John 4:8

FORGIVENESS
Psalms 103:12
Matthew 11:25
Ephesians 4:31-32
1 John 1:9

CHILDREN/FERTILITY
Genesis 49:25
Exodus 201:12
1 Samuel 1:27
Jeremiah 32:27

HER PRAYERS

"A woman who kneels before God, can stand before anyone or anything."

Celi Marie Dean-Touré

HER PRAISES

"Enter his gates with thanksgiving and his courts with praise; give thanks to him and praise his name. For the Lord is good and his love endures forever; his faithfulness continues through all generations."

Psalms 100:4-5

HER INTERCESSIONS

HER DREAMS

> *"Now to Him who is able to do exceedingly abundantly above all that we ask or think, according to the power that works in us…"*
>
> Ephesians 3:20

HER VISIONS

"Write the vision
And make it plain on tablets,
That he may run who reads it.
For the vision is yet for an
appointed time;
But at the end it will speak, and it
will not lie.
Though it tarries, wait for it,
Because it will surely come, It will
not tarry."
Habakkuk 2:2-3

"Little girls with dreams become women with vision."
Unknown

"God is within her, she will not fail."
Psalms 46:5

"I dream it, I work hard, I grind till I own it."
Beyoncé

"She is more precious than rubies,
  And all the things you may desire cannot compare with her."
    Proverbs 3:15

"My mission in life is not merely to survive, but to thrive; and to do so with some passion, some compassion, some humor, and some style"

Maya Angelou

"Strength and honor are her clothing; She shall rejoice in time to come."
  Proverbs 31:25

"For I know the thoughts that I think toward you, says the Lord, thoughts of peace and not of evil, to give you a future and a hope."
Jeremiah 29:11

"God created you on purpose, for a purpose and
He never wants fear of the unexpected to hold you back."
Christine Caine

"She opens her mouth with wisdom, And on her tongue is the law of kindness."
Proverbs 31:26

"Charm is deceitful and beauty is passing,
But a woman who fears the Lord, she shall be praised.
Give her of the fruit of her hands,
And let her own works praise her in the gates."
Proverbs 31:30-31

"For me, becoming isn't about arriving somewhere or achieving a certain aim.
I see it instead as forward motion, a means of evolving,
a way to reach continuously toward a better self.
The journey doesn't end."
Michelle Obama

"I can do all things through Christ who strengthens me."
Philippians 4:13

"She exchanged her fears for God's favor."
Lisa Bevere

"You will also declare a thing,
And it will be established for you; So light will shine on your ways."
Job 22:28

"I have chosen to no longer be apologetic for my femaleness and my femininity. And I want to be respected in all of my femaleness because I deserve to be."

Chimamanda Ngozi Adichie

"And my God shall supply all your need according to His riches in glory by Christ Jesus."
Philippians 4:19

"Every woman's success should be an inspiration to another.
We're strongest when we cheer each other on."
Serena Williams

"And we know that all things work together for good to those who love God, to those who are the called according to His purpose."
Romans 8:28

"I may not be where I want to be, but thank God I am not where I used to be."

Joyce Meyer

"Be still, and know that I am God."
Psalms 46:10